NOTES ON BUSINESS

The Music of Business and the Business of Music

VIC HYLAND

Notes on Business

First published 2012

Published by 440 music Ltd

Rosewood House High Street Hadlow Kent TN11 0EF

Email: vichyland@teachmusic.co.uk Phone: 01732 850995

URL: http://www.bluescampuk.co.uk

Photographs by Rohan Troy

Printed by Lulu

Notes on Business – the music of business and the business of music

Hyland Vic

ISBN 978-0-9572840-0-5

Contents

FORWARD

As someone who has spent most of their life running or working for businesses from
the smallest to international concerns I am aware that clear thought on what you need
to do is essential. An obvious problem is that most of us get caught up in the adrenalin
rush and enthusiasm of a new enterprise or idea. That's fine and all part of the game,
but you do need to focus on what is actually going to work and turn that into decisions
and action. It's for this reason that there are a plethora of business self-help books and
a raft of people searching for the one that inspires them. You have hopefully just
found the one for you.

Vic Hyland has been a friend for many years. I got to know him as a rock music fan
and his excellent skill as a musician fronting his band. In addition to being a first class
guitarist of the Clapton school, he has always taken a keen interest in personal
development. He has had various small business interests, but has not been a 'Captain
of Industry' by any stretch of the imagination. So why should he be giving you life
and business guidance? Well, I remember many years ago organising a world class
extreme endurance sports event and the Daily Mail chief sports correspondent Neil
Wilson asking at the launch press conference how the hell I thought I could be the
event director when I had never done any extreme distance event beyond being a mid
field London marathon punter. I pointed out my skill was in the organising not the
participation...two very different things. The same applies to Vic, his skill in this book
is to reach out to people with simple and clear ideas of what getting on in your work
life requires, whether starting a small company or improving your career. He knows
that world and understands what it takes. Most importantly he provides a novel and
entertaining perspective using the analogy of how to make a success in a band as his
way in to the wider picture. I am sure this will appeal to those of us who find so many
other such lifestyle and work enhancement books dull and dry in the extreme. So
'rock up' and enjoy the Vic Hyland take on making your working life more successful
and, more importantly, more enjoyable.

Nick Jenkins

INTRODUCTION

Like countless others, I had a dream – the dream of playing guitar in a band. This continued unresolved until my wife, fed up with my three-chord repertoire, bought guitar lessons for my birthday – to 'get it out of my system'. However, what emerged became the stress buster, the hobby and the connection that seemed to make sense of things.

I had a couple of friends who wanted to start a band, so the great journey to rock-and-roll heaven began: the fans, the gigs, the recordings . . . OK, the rehearsals in smelly rooms and the gigs in the crap pubs but, hey. we were paying our dues.

One thing we were missing was a bass player and that turned out to be the most important addition that was to happen.
Pete, the drummer, knew this old guy called Grant who had played bass in bands for years. He was rather sage-like and only spoke when he deemed it necessary; otherwise he would let us get on with it, making our mistakes and learning from them.

The other completely unexpected side to all of this was that my 'other' life, as a businessman, seemed to be shadowing the development of the band and its lessons. This is the story.

Chapter 1

LEARNING TO LISTEN

Hi. My name is Joe. At this point in the story, I play guitar – not brilliantly, but well enough to be in a band (whatever that means). I have two good friends who also play, Mike on guitar and Pete on drums. The three of us had jammed around – with me on vocals because no one else would sing (I was the only one mad enough to have a go) – but we were just missing the bass player. Occasionally Mike covered on bass but we really needed someone to 'to hold down the groove' and that is when Grant came into the picture.

Pete had known Grant for some time but, because Grant was a seasoned pro, Pete didn't at first ask if he would be interested in joining us; but, as happens, something was mentioned in conversation and Grant said he would help us out – so in he came.

When not playing, Grant was quietly watchful. However, as time went on, although he never interfered with our process of learning by trial and error, every now and again he would give us a pearl of wisdom. That was when I noticed that the same lesson would crop up in my business - weird though that may sound: life imitating art.

I was a bit nervous about playing with this guy who seemed to have played with some big names; but he was so quiet, getting information out of him about his past was like getting blood out of a stone. He would just smile and turn the conversation to what we were doing. Only later did we realised he had dodged the questions.

Then came the first rehearsal with the full band. The most memorable part of it occurred when we got lost in the middle of the first number and the song just fell apart. We proceeded to do what we normally did, which was to argue about who had done what and what should have happened.

After five minutes or so of this, we noticed that Grant was standing on one side, smiling, so Pete said 'OK, Grant, what do you think we should do?'

Grant shut his eyes for a moment and then said, 'Some of this band are only listening to themselves, which means they are playing too loud and are unaware of the others. One of you *is* listening to the others but, when they go wrong, so does he.'

That left us slightly puzzled. I asked, 'So, if we are not supposed to be listening to ourselves *or* others, what are we supposed to be listening to?'

'The groove', Grant replied succinctly, looking me straight in the eye.

'Right,' I glanced round at the others who were clearly as confused as I was. 'And where is 'the groove?'

'In the spaces between the people', said Grant. 'By listening to the combined sounds of the music, it will talk to you, through your mind, and you will get the feel of it. And what is so cool about this is there is no effort involved.'

All this stuff was easier said than done but, after a while, it seemed to click and I began to see and feel what he meant. Within a few weeks, it was as if my default setting had changed so that, even when I listened to music at home or in the car, I started to register elements in familiar songs that I had had not noticed before, weird.

<table>
<tr><td colspan="2">THE BAND</td></tr>
<tr><td>♫</td><td>Joe – guitar and vocals</td></tr>
<tr><td>♫</td><td>Mike – guitar and keyboards</td></tr>
<tr><td>♫</td><td>Pete – drums</td></tr>
<tr><td>♫</td><td>Grant – bass guitar</td></tr>
</table>

LISTENING TO THE SPACES

I hate giving presentations and I have tried lots of things – to no avail - that are supposed to help build confidence, such as picturing people sitting in front of me in their underwear. Unfortunately for me, if it's good-looking women who are sitting there, that just makes things worse.

A few days after the band rehearsal, I had a presentation that I knew would be difficult. Possibly because I had some knowledge of the people who would be in the room, I felt that I should try the idea of working the spaces between the people and searching for 'the groove'. Also while exploring this idea; I had heard an interview with a comedian who had said that his technique of dealing with an audience was to look at the spaces between the people and not directly at their faces.

At first it seemed rather odd. I was sure people would suss what I was doing but they seemed to relax and listen. I was more aware than usual of the facial expressions and the body language of the people in the room and yet I was somehow detached from them and just 'going with it'.

I had several realisations in that meeting, one of which was that I was previously always listening to myself. I also became aware of others in the room who mirrored what their superiors said, just listening to them and not themselves.

This was very strange. To think that I had never been aware of this before – maybe because I had played the same game. What was also very powerful, this time, was that I could see everyone's viewpoints overlaid and, although I might not agree with them, I could see how each person had arrived at their opinions. I was picking up the 'feel' of the mood of the whole room.

From this new vantage point, I explained what I could clearly see was their situation and I said that I would go away, find a solution to the problems raised and then would contact within two to three days with my new proposal.

I left the meeting feeling confident and very buoyant, even though an agreement had not yet been reached, I worked through all the points raised until, within a few days, we had reached an agreement that satisfied all of us.

What really impacted on me was the feeling and experience that came with my shift in perspective and how I was receiving information, nothing else seemed different at first– just me. Then, somehow, my shift created a change in others. Maybe because I seemed more receptive it lowered barriers, or perhaps it changed the chemistry between us in the room.

Chapter 2

PLAY WITH INTENTION; BE THE ROCK GOD

The rehearsals seemed to be going well and we almost had a set for a gig when Pete suggested that we should video ourselves to see what the punters were going to get – which, it turned out, was *really* bad! The band members were staring at the floor, sometimes with their backs to the 'audience' – a classic bunch of middle-aged men looking embarrassed whilst playing musical instruments. The exception was Grant; he was just playing and in the flow with the music.

'OK, so what do we need to do to fix this travesty of "a cool band"?' I asked Grant.

'Play with intention, play with attitude; remember, people need to believe in you. To them you are the Shaman, the Witchdoctor; the Hootchie Coochie Man. If you do not believe that you are the Rock God, how will you convince anyone else?' Grant said.

'I know, but I would feel stupid doing that.'

'Well,' said Grant, 'you might feel stupid because this is different to what you are used to doing, but you won't look any worse than you do at the moment! Just do it and we will film it.'

Then, as we were about to kick into the song, Grant whispered in my left ear, 'Think of a time when you played a song as you stood in front of a mirror and pretended to be someone famous'.

I thought of teenage days spent standing before the bedroom mirror pretending to be Jimi Hendrix playing 'Voodoo Chile'.

I heard Grant saying, 'That's right', and felt his hand touch my shoulder as we started to play. 'Now make the feeling twice as big'.

For the most part, I managed to keep up the Rock God routine. It did feel odd and I left the 'stage' unconvinced; but, in the next playback, I came over ten times better and so did the rest of the band - and we were clearly having fun.

'That was amazing! How did that happen?' asked Pete.

'It's rather like the concept of all the clocks in a room ticking in time; it's about resonance. "Fake it, until you make it",' he went on to say. 'And what you saw in the second video is what the audience will see as well.'

'Cool,' said Mike. 'It obviously looked good, but why did it feel so odd when we were acting out the Rock God stuff?

Grant smiled: 'When you were doing that, you were emptying the cup so you could pour something else in there. You had to step out of your old zone to make room for the new. The confusion and discomfort came from that emptiness.'

Pete got up. 'Come on, let's have another go. We have got to get used to the cameras if we are going to be stars.'

SELL WITH INTENTION

Like many entrepreneurs, I have fingers in lots of pies, little business ideas – some that run and some that do not– of these many involve selling.

I have often been puzzled as to why some things sell and others do not. Often, the fast-selling items are crap while the demand for really good products or services may inexplicably wither on the vine.

It seems to be true that, when I am busy, work flows in like a torrent and, when I have to say 'Sorry, I am too busy,' clients become even more interested and adamant that they want me to do the job. When the work tails off, and I begin to feel a bit desperate, the opposite seems to happen. People seem to be able to smell it and I know I won't even get a look in.

So, for a little project that I was working on, I created the mental intention that I was in demand. My belief and attitude was: 'Play with intention, be the Sales God' I cultivated a swagger, had the suit pressed, cleaned up my act and followed Grant's Rock God instructions. I shut my eyes and thought of a time when the sale went really well and then got the feeling and made it bigger and moved 'into the zone'.

That day was a dream. People appeared quite different. We chatted and they made orders, it was so relaxed and it all seemed in complete contrast to those too-frequent days when I feel as if I am pushing a peanut up a hill. This time I was coasting downhill with the breeze in my hair.

Over the next couple of weeks people were phoning to say a friend had recommended me and that they were interested in my sending details or popping into see them. How good is that!

Have you ever tried to sell something that you do not believe in? It is difficult to pull off unless you can find something to focus on. Look at the great entrepreneurs; they exude confidence about what they are selling because they believe in what they are doing. This time I had learnt that you can make this happen by just creating that image for yourself.

And apart from being rewarding and successful, it was fun. I could hear Grant's voice following me around, saying 'Just jam with the idea man!'.

Chapter 3

PUTTING LIFE INTO YOUR MUSIC.

I spent a few weeks learning the solo from 'Give Me All Your Loving' by ZZ Top
and then, during the next rehearsal, we played the song. However when we got to the
solo section, and I played what I had learned, although it sounded OK, it felt too much
as if I was 'going through the motions'.

'You need a bit more soul in there,' said Grant. 'Why don't you just improvise
something, make it fresh? You don't have to stick to the original lead guitar solo.'

So we did it again, with me just rambling around the scale. This time it sounded
worse!

Grant stopped us. 'You need to speak through the guitar. Make the notes have the
rhythms of your language. In your head, say something, anything - what you had for
breakfast, what you saw on TV - and then say it in time with the music. Putting the
notes to the words will breathe life into the solo.'

I did as he said and, after a while, things started to feel better. Then, I played an
idea from the original song, but with a slightly different rhythm, which slotted in well
and sounded really good.

'Good. Now, here is the 'cool' thing. Allow the song to link you to a to a memory
or a fantasy - in this case something a little bit soulful and sexy - and say the things
that would be said in your fantasy. Let the words and the emotion flow through'

When we ran through it the next time I felt like a chump at first but, when I let
go, something happened; something supercharged!

Grant stopped us and the band looked at me: 'That was fantastic.' said Mike; 'It
made the hairs on the back of my neck stand up!'

'Well done', said Grant. 'You cannot separate the mind and its thoughts or your
feelings from your body language so, if you think about something, it will come
through your playing because it comes out through your body. And because we are
all, in effect, radio sets, as you are sending out these feelings, so they are being picked
up by the receivers of your listener.'

'Hey are we doing telepathy?' I quipped.

Grant looked serious and nodded his head; 'Yes that is what goes on in a band; that is how the rhythm section works; that is how I know what type of roll the drummer is going to play and when the guitarist is going to launch into a solo. I even know which girl in the front row the lead vocalist fancies!

'That is how our ancestors survived, by "reading" people and situations – and we still do it. We "read" body language and environments without having to think about it; it's programmed in.

'The essence of playing great music is not to believe but to become, in the same way as an actor gets into character. In order to play great music you must breathe it and speak it.'

We ran through the idea again until I felt I had really grasped it. There was still work to be done but I was beginning to be able to move in and out of character as the song dictated. And was that a buzz!

GETTING THE MESSAGE ACROSS.

I have often pondered on the notion that, if you smiled sweetly at someone you thought was a waste of time, the smile might not work because your mind was loudly transmitting the idea that they were an idiot. Would those thoughts appear so strongly on your face or in your body language that the idiot was bound to pick them up?

Going by what Grant had said, this might be the case, and might explain why, even when I was extra nice to people I disliked, my charm offensive still didn't work. Perhaps I should change my approach. Better to keep a positive picture in my mind and say pleasant things while I smiled sweetly at them.

This might also solve the enigma of the way that work flows into a business. I had often wondered why, when I was busy, the business just kept coming in; yet when things got quiet and I had to tout for business, it was much harder to get. Now, I know there could be lots of reasons for this but, I had the feeling that, somewhere in my voice, was a hidden message that wailed, 'Listen! I am desperate! Give me the contract!'

I started to rethink how I might do business; for instance, maybe changing the image that I had of the outcome might help. Interestingly, this seemed to make sense 'deep down'; after all, if you are planning a journey, you needed to have a clear idea of where you are going.

In the following days, I noticed that, by using these techniques I could enhance all my ways and means of communicating with people. Conversely, I started to see that other people would often say one thing and that their tone of voice, body language etc would be saying the opposite. In one case, a client was telling me that they liked an idea while subtly shaking their head and pulling a face as if they were chewing a wasp.

I thought carefully about my previous modes of communication, recognising how often my actions did not mirror my conversation but gave away my true feelings.

I could now see how great musicians could connect with an authentic feeling that their song then carried to the listener. Of course, if this is true of music then it must also be true of language.

The more I looked for the hidden elements in peoples' conversational programming, the more obvious they became. All the time, people are leaking information through their choice of words, tonality and, of course, body language. We pick this up unconsciously; however, when you are conscious of this you can use it to inform your judgement with the information coming from what you are really seeing and hearing.

I now see that the mystery of why, in the past, I did not do well in some negotiations or interviews may have been down to my not communicating effectively.

Chapter 4

BEING A FRONT MAN

We spent time running through the numbers and then watching ourselves on video to see how we could improve.

Looking at one of these playbacks, I noticed something interesting. I looked to be playing as if I wasn't any part of the session, on top of which the song seemed 'disjointed', but I could not work out what was wrong.

As I was standing there in some frustration, Grant looked at me and asked 'Are you OK?'

'No, I seem to be playing rubbish, as if it's all not happening, somehow; almost as if I am in a different place from the rest of the band,' I replied

Grant smiled and suggested we take the song right back to basics. So, starting with the drums and the bass, he filtered through everything, cut out the drum fills and then added the guitars and the vocals and, hey presto! it sounded really good.

The difference was amazing. The song now felt more relaxed and flowed really well. Grant suggested that we play through it again and, as we did, the disjointedness reappeared. There was a drum fill – and then the song lost it's groove again.

'Stop,' said Grant; 'Pete, that roll was slightly out of time and that's what's throwing everything slightly off. You will need to keep it all very simple until you have nailed the timing.'

Grant looked at me: 'The problem with being the front man is that, when anything goes wrong in the rhythm section, you look like the one who has made a mistake. Frequently, errors in the rhythm section are so subtle that it seems that *you* are the one not playing well; it's only when you listen back that you will spot what's going wrong.'

Grant went on to stress that the rhythm section is the engine room of the band and, no matter how well a singer or lead player is performing, they won't sound good if the engine room isn't doing its job.

'Could it happen that you had a rather average singer but that, with a strong rhythm section, they could sound better?' I asked

'I would say that, with a good rhythm section, if the singer up front responds to what the band is doing and works off that, he or she will become a much better performer. So, in a word, yes, but only if they are responsive to the band.

Over the next few weeks, I noticed that Pete's drumming became tighter and the rolls and fills that he was doing were much better – as if he was growing in confidence and technique. Then I learned that Grant had been working with him.

So, the band was going from being a bunch of older boys with toys to a proper outfit that could play publicly without causing itself or the audience any embarrassment. This was exciting!

BEING A GOOD SALESMAN IS SOMETIMES NOT ENOUGH

Bob has been a good friend for a number of years and he is one of the best salesmen that I know. He could sell you your own watch. His brain is hard-wired to finding the key features of a product, eliciting which of those could offer the benefits that you are looking for – and then seamlessly sell them to you.

However, things were not going too well for Bob. We were sitting over a beer, one lunch time, and he was telling me that, since the company had expanded, the delivery of goods was not up to the usual high standard and this had been causing him problems.

Bob had received calls from customers irritated that either the whole order had not arrived or that they had received the wrong items. He lamented the fact that all the errors of the warehouse and the office staff always made him look like the one at fault.

'Well, mate,' I said sagely, 'that always happens to the front man if the guys at the back make a mistake. The audience always think it is you.'

'Yes, and you can't turn round and blame the staff because that reflects just as badly on you; you have to take it squarely on the chin. I'm not sure how you deal with this because it seems to be endemic now: the company has grown too fast and the correct checks and balances are not in place. What worked for the small company doesn't seem to work for the bigger company and they will either need to invest or find some way of getting the processes right.'

'Maybe,' I offered, 'it's training that's needed; maybe the warehouse people need to go out on the road with you to see, first hand, who the customers are.'

'Good point, but some of these guys seem to be so thick or else they think the world owes them a living – or maybe both!' Bob look out of the window. 'Many appear to be unaware that their mistakes could cause the company to fail because they are not working as part of a team. It doesn't matter where you are in the organisation, everyone needs to take pride in their work and, if they make a mistake, they need to 'fess up to it and then fix it so it doesn't happen again.'

'Maybe you need to change your rhythm section?' I suggested.

'Change the what?' asked Bob.

'Oh, nothing. It is just a term I use for the back-room people who should be holding it all together and giving the company its drive through focused customer service.'

Bob laughed: 'Blimey, mate, how many corporate training courses have you been on recently?'

Chapter 5

WHEN DOES THE SHOW START AND FINISH?

We had the possibility of a gig at a friend's party. This would be our first outing.

Mike suggested that we should go to see another friend's band, which was performing in the village hall, and look out for any performance ideas that might be good for us.

The most significant thing about that gig happened right at the beginning of the set. This is not to say they were bad, merely rather as you would expect a friends band to be. However, as the lights went down and they came onto the stage, one of them tripped over. He got up, dusted himself off and carried on as if nothing happened. The next day, the highlight of the gig was his undignified entry.

Grant hadn't been with us, so we were relating this story to him and having a bit of a laugh about it. He nodded and smiled but later pointed out that there was a lesson in it for us.

'The show starts before you arrive on stage. As musicians we forget this because we are focusing on the playing and not the audience experience. Think about what has to happen before you start playing. You come on stage, plug in the guitars, find your way over to the drum stool or get ready to play that first keyboard riff – and all with no lights! Getting on stage can be a perfectly straightforward task, but nerves can make it a difficult one. You need plenty of extra practice in order to be certain which person goes first and who goes last. Remember, you need to be able to do this in the dark and with nerves added to the mix.

'You will have the same problem at the end of the concert when, again, everybody has get offstage in a professional manner. This is just general stagecraft, but is often left out of the performance practise. There was a conductor who once said that as long as you start together and finish together nobody gives a damn what goes on in the middle.'

So we started working on getting on and off the stage, plugging and unplugging the equipment, making sure that the set flowed and ensuring that the audience would experience a fluent professional performance.

Grant explained that bands often missed things that seemed unimportant to them but had the capacity to destroy all the good work of the performance – including being rude to people and being drunk on stage.

We felt, after that rehearsal, that the band moved up a gear or two and that we were ready to test ourselves in the bear pit of a live performance. OK that's a bit of an exaggeration – at our mate's party.

SELLING YOURSELF BEFORE YOU ARRIVE AND AFTER YOU HAVE LEFT

I found I was bringing to mind, more and more often, various incidents that had occurred since Pete, Mike, Grant and I had got together in a band, each of which had been the basis of one of Grant's 'How to be a better band' lessons.

I was reflecting, now, on the guy who tripped up as he came on stage at the start of his band's gig, and feeling that there seemed to be a lesson that I could draw for my life from this and our other recent musical experiences.

I thought over various business presentations I had given in the past and wondered whether I had destroyed my chances before I even got into the boardroom.

Before any presentation, you have to make your way through the building, meeting people at all stages of your journey to the room you are to use. There are many opportunities for 'tripping over' before the presentation starts; maybe the first slip-up came when you chose your tie for the day.

A number of examples that came back to mind made me feel rather uncomfortable and I also noticed that, often, I did not seem to be especially successful at those events.

I became more aware of the damage that can be caused to your business by being careless before and after a sale.

For instance, someone makes a decision about whether they like you or not within the first four seconds of seeing you. Hence the importance of what you wear: clothes set the mood.

The context that surrounds the idea and it's presentation is also very important and this could be where the meeting is, what you language you use and what you look like. Context effects the unconscious, slipping into the mind unnoticed while we are listening to the words being used.

Now, when I practised the content of my presentations, I included entering the building *and* the allocated room *and* getting up to the front to speak, and then how I finished and how I leave the building.

I started to wonder about whether Grant understood how those ideas could be used in other areas or whether he even cared as he seemed rather a laid back hippie that the business world would be an anathema to him.

Chapter 6

THE FIRST GIG. IT'S PARTY TIME.

The date for our first 'booking' came around very quickly and, although it was only a friend's party, nerves were beginning to show amongst the rock novices. We rehearsed the songs till we had so 'honed them to the bone' that they were getting a little boring.

On the day of the gig, we set up in the afternoon, organising the equipment and borrowing a bigger vocal PA system than we normally use for practise. When we then ran through a number to sound check, Grant pointed out that, as we were playing to an empty marquee, a rough balance of sound was enough. When it filled up with people, the sound would change anyway.

The nerves for the build-up to this, our first short set in front of a crowd – even if only friends – were gut-churning. I reminded myself that I do far more important things without getting anything like as worked up!

The set went well and seemed to be over in a flash. We were really buzzing and the crowd loved us, so we did an encore. However, they still wanted more and we gave them a number that we had only recently started working on. Well, we got lost: the song fell apart and we had to abandon it. Fortunately, our 'home crowd' seemed to think this was fun and it didn't sour the evening.

At the end of the set, Mike, Pete and I went outside. We were chatting about how good it had all been when Grant appeared, beer in hand.

'What do you think, mate, did we rock the house?' asked Pete

'Yes, you did well,' Grant acknowledged – adding 'for a first gig in front of friends.'

That remark certainly took some of the wind out of my sails, but I saw that he had a point.

'You did make one mistake, though: you should always leave them wanting more. The last number was unnecessary, but that is good learning for you.'

'What about playing to people who are not our friends, how different is that?'

'Very different; first off, you will have to connect with them and, secondly, you'll have to be ready for some of them to think you are crap, because people are very opinionated when it comes to music.'

'So, what next, mister bass man?' asked Pete.

'Two gigs, both in pubs: one where you bring in your crowd and one where you don't. Then – learn from that.' Grant finished his beer, said good night and disappeared.

I reflected on all that had happened before and during our first 'appearance'. We had worked hard for it and, generally, it went very well. Afterwards, we watched a video of the gig and it was OK, but not as good as we remembered. Perhaps being outside of the emotion of the live performance, and seeing it in the cold light of day, gave us a reality check.

When someone comes up with an idea, family and friends will very often say (or even think) it is good because they want to be encouraging – and don't want to be insulting – and that may well give a false sense of its worth. When you get into the outside world no one has a vested interest in you and that's when the idea has to stand on its own merits.

When it comes to business activities that involve a performance – as in the selling of goods or services or talents (e.g. music) – Grant summed up the matter well when he said: 'Your real challenge is the audience of people who don't know you from Adam. If you can make them like you, you're on to a winner.'

Also, at the gig, we did overstay our welcome; we should have left when the going was good. The golden rule is 'Leave on a high', which is certainly true in the case of business.

One of the positives from this first gig was that a number of friends said we were much better than they expected – again, equally important in business. Make sure that you over-deliver; make the product better than the customers were expecting because then they will pass the word to others.

I know that, in the past, I was not prepared enough before going out to sell or launch a new idea. And what about the audience that I was selling to? Often I knew nothing about them – what they would like, how they would respond. Trying to sell yourself to someone who does not like the business song that you sing is, quite frankly, impossible.

With the passing of time, I was discovering a lot about myself and my business and ideas that needed a new perspective.

No one likes to be hurt, no one likes to be told, 'No, sorry, not today', or 'We are not using you any more, we are switching to another supplier/brand because you are not good enough (or not cheap enough)'.

Successful business is often about a deep connection between something in the mind of the buyer and that of the seller. People would rather buy from someone they like.

It was going to be interesting to see what would be thrown up by our next project.

Chapter 7

DOING THE PUB GIG

The next project was to put three songs onto a demo CD that we send to pubs and clubs in the area in order to generate some interest in the band. The plan was, as Grant had suggested, testing the set out in front of crowds that were not so familiar to us.

As luck would have it, before we did any recording we managed to pick up a gig when another band was forced to cancel a date. We arrived at the Queens Head pub, unloaded the gear and set up. We were stuck in a corner of the pub almost blocking the door to the toilets and, as we had never played in such a small space before, the evening was spent trying not to knock each other out with our guitars.

The gig went well and a few friends turned up but, generally, the crowd was made up of the locals who appeared to like us, apart from one guy who thought we were too loud. The landlord was pleased and wanted us back as the takings for the evening were good, and people were certainly drinking and having fun.

Several things struck me about the evening. Firstly, a couple of numbers in the set that went down really well were songs that I do not particularly like, but others obviously do; and, interestingly enough, one song that went down a storm was one I thought we had played rather badly.

Grant was hanging around the bar talking to the landlord. They were clearly old friends.

'How was that for you?' he asked me.

'Yes, I think it went well; the punters seemed to like it,' I said

'Yes indeed, it seemed fine. You see,' he continued, 'I always go on what the audience likes. I have had times when I think I have played well but then someone who has seen us many times before will say, "Why did you play such and such?", which actually means: "That was rubbish, you should ditch that song". Or they may say, "That was the best you have ever played that number", when you thought it was total crap. You see, my friend, beauty is in the ear or, should I say, the gut of the beholder. If they feel good, then it is good and, let's face it, if you are being paid then what the punter likes is the key to what you play and what you leave out.'

This was said with such passion I really felt it was a lesson learnt over and over again, almost an undeniable truth.

I packed away the gear and said goodbye to all and set off home. It had been a tiring evening but I was still buzzing. I can see why the after-gig party is the rock'n'roll thing – because sleep is impossible when you are on such a buzz, and we had only played a pokey little pub! Imagine what a big festival would feel like!

Eventually, I slipped into a deep sleep and started dreaming about being late for an important stadium concert because the local vicar had borrowed my helicopter. My unconscious was processing something, but I am not sure what.

THE TRUE VALUE OF CROWD FEELING.

Many years back, my father worked for a company that sold the early video machines. The shop was selling the two formats available at the time, one was called Betamax and the other one was VHS. Betamax was regarded by many as the better machine, but, for some reason, it was completely outsold by its rival. Eventually, Betamax sank without trace and VHS was left as the only format for video.

There are many instances where this has happened, which seems to prove false the old adage: 'If you make a better mousetrap, the world will beat a path to your door'.

The key to success lies in the decisions of the general public and these are not based on an intellectual process but more of a 'gut' reaction. The more you think about it, the more examples there are.

In the early days of personal computing, Apple Computers near lost out to the PC format and it took many years for the Mac to achieve a safe place in the market. In fact, what eventually happened was that the biggest name in the PC market place, IBM, got out of the production side of the PC. This proved a shrewd move in the end, because of all the cheap competition, but it also allowed Apple to capitalise on the design, uniqueness and the reliability of its own machines.

I could see, now, that getting up in front of an unfamiliar crowd was vital to finding out what people really thought as friends tend to be too polite. People who do not know you can be brutally honest.

You can easily deceive yourself, over a 'good idea', if you seek the opinion of close friends or, worse still, family members. You need to get outside people in from the outset to help assess an idea. When you have invested a lot of time and energy in something, you fall in love with it and of course 'love is blind'; so an unbiased viewpoint is essential.

The other aspect often overlooked is the environmental factor. The pub that we played in was very small and we had to function in that space, and it was not a space that I would have chosen but the only one that was available. That is a problem faced by new products – they are often not suitable, in some way, for their supposed market and they lack the adaptability to overcome that.

Think of how many times you have bought something that did not have the right connecting lead to fit the equipment that you already owned and, of course, you did not discover this until you got the product home. Or something breaks down on a computer, such as the power unit, and, because you have had it for a while, you cannot get that type any longer, so you have to buy a new computer. Not very eco-friendly and it creates a lot for bad feeling towards the product.

Remember that the customer is king and, if the king does not like it, your head will roll.

Chapter 8

PREPARING FOR THE RECORDING SESSION

We were going to record some songs in order to get some gigs in the pubs which Grant had recommended, but first we needed to work on the songs.

We went into the next rehearsal to find Grant had organised the room so we could not see one another. He also made us first play the songs through with just bass and drums and then with other variations of instruments added after the rhythm section was right.

This was very new. Suddenly we did not know where we were in a song because it sounded so different. Usual cues, such as the lyrics, were not there so we had to know our parts really well.

Grant suggested that we only need three songs for the demo, songs chosen to reflect the variety of our output. We could play them straight, as if we are gigging, but it might best for us to multitrack in order to get a better balance of sound.

Multitracking means that the recording happens in layers, usually drums and bass followed by guitar and keyboards with the vocals and lead solos on last. The problem for us was how, as we did not usually play that way.

Today's recording with computers means there are some things are easier and others more difficult than using the analogue recordings of the old tape machines. However, as long as we knew what we wanted as a finished product, then, under Grant's guidance, we could decide how to prepare for such a result.

Grant told us lots of stories about famous recordings from the past. He talked about Elvis and the recordings that he made at Sun Studios. These were all made from straight takes; they simply recorded one after another and then chose the best. Grant played us some recordings of the guitarist Les Paul and his singer wife Mary Ford: these were the first serious examples of multitracking. They sounded incredible, particularly when you realised that some of the parts were recorded in a hotel room.

We listened to the stories of the recordings at Abbey Road with the Beatles and at the Rolling Stones' Mobile Studio and the recordings of Tamla Motown and Led Zeppelin – all the way through to stories from the present day. What he stressed to us was some of the best ideas were simple but the most important thing was to have the end in sight. 'Know your outcome' he said.

We came up with the idea of breaking the song down and making a guide recording of me singing to a drum beat while Grant marked out the structure of the song with such cues as 'Guitar solo and chorus coming up'. This would help the others through their performances as they rebuilt the song in layers.

'Also, guys you will need a few hours on another day to mix the recording. A few days after you've got over the euphoria of playing, you can listen to the songs in the cold light of day and then decide on the complete mix.

'You've already learned a lot from looking back at the video of a gig. It was not as good as you thought it would be, right?'
Some things are best using the unconscious and being in the flow and other things are better when you purely analytical like mixing the track.

PREPARING FOR A PRODUCT LAUNCH.

Fired up by our preparations for doing a studio recording with the band, I decided to use some of what we'd been learning to make an online video to demonstrate some camping equipment that I was looking to sell.

A little while ago I had bought some stock from a camping shop that was closing down and I managed to get a good deal on various items such tents and camping stoves. These items had been sitting in store for a while and I decided to create an online video so that I could demonstrate the items for sale.

I went onto YouTube and checked out various videos and took notes on what seemed to work and what didn't. I looked at videos that had clocked up lots of viewings and tried to work out how they had been done and what gave them their appeal.

It was during a session of sitting in a café, scribbling down ideas, when who should walk by but Grant. I caught his eye and signalled to him to come in.

'Hi man, what are you doing?' Grant said as he sat down.

'I am working on an idea for a YouTube clip to promote sales,' I said.

'Cool,' Grant nodded his head

'But I am stuck,' I said. 'It seems that things can be very simple – and very cheap to do – but I am not sure where to start on this.'

'Think of how we broke the song down. Then, to rebuild it, we had to find the thread that ran through it. With the recording, that is your vocal, plus a backing beat and maybe a guitar – and this is the guide. Well, you need a theme that runs through the video.'

I shut my eyes to see or feel if I had any sense of my 'guide'. As I did so, I heard Grant's voice say, 'That's right, just relax and let the idea fall into pieces and then allow them to drift *down* to the ground. As you watch them float *down*, some of them will seem more important, as if they are the things that are the key.'

This was weird because I did see lots of leaves floating down, but some of them lit up and the other leaves then seemed to cluster around. It was a 'eureka' moment where everything seemed obvious. I could even see the film in my head.

Grant's voice continued, 'Just take it *piece* by *piece* and the *rest* will follow.'

For a moment, I don't know what happened. I seemed to fall asleep, maybe for a few seconds, and then I heard a voice say, 'Have you finished?' I looked up and the waitress was standing there: 'Have you finished with your cup?'

Grant was grinning. I had fallen asleep, I seemed to have a plan in my head about the way this video was going to fit together, I grabbed a pen and started writing.

'Can I have another coffee please?' The waitress looked at me as if I was some sort of nut.

'Have I been asleep?' I said

'I guess so, you were snoring loudly.' Grant chuckled.

'Sorry about that. I was doing some creative thinking.' I smiled at the waitress.

'Oh,' she said raising her head in a puzzled gesture, looking at Grant

'I must have bored him to sleep.' Grant looked me straight in the eye and raised an eyebrow.

Chapter 9

RECORDING SESSION

We felt like a real rock band going into the studio to do our first recording and, because we were prepared, we quickly got the drums abd bass down and started building up the guitar tracks.

Grant and the engineer steered us through the order of things, encouraging us to work in a various ways for different parts of the recording. When there was a 'take', they had to settle us all down and find ways of relaxing us because we were so nervous about being recorded. I felt my fingers become lumps of wood and the simplest things became difficult.

When I heard myself back, isolated from the band, I became aware of all the mistakes and bum notes which had got lost in the mix when we were playing live. I realised I would need to brush up on all aspects of my playing. Grant was reassuring; he said there were lots of examples of wrong notes and out-of-tune instruments on some of the all-time classics and what was important was the overall sound at the end.

We redid the vocal and Grant showed me a good trick to 'get in the groove', as he put it. I was to turn off the lights and imagine myself as the original singer and visualise the video that would be the promo for the song. This took my mind off the technicalities of the song and into the performance; it just made it seem more fluent somehow.

At the end of the day, the sound guys did a rough mix, which we were each given a copy of to take away and listen to, and a date was set for the final mix.

I was knackered. I don't know if it was the concentration on the music or the electrical equipment causing some form of energy drain but I needed to clear my head.

I went outside and sat down with the others. Everyone agreed they felt the same, totally exhausted but very excited by the recording. It had sounded great.

'Maybe, though, when we listen back to it tomorrow, it will sound rubbish like the video of the gig did,' said Pete.

'Some of this stuff really seems to screw up your brain. I guess it's better not to intellectualise but just go with the flow: feel and not think,' said Mike.

'That is exactly what I'd realised,' I said. 'I was beginning to believe I was loosing my marbles.' I told them about what happened in the coffee shop.

Pete laughed: 'I didn't tell you that Grant has done this sort of thing to me before. He seems to have some weird power –like a kind of hypnosis – but, if you ask him about it, he just gives you one of his grins after telling you he doesn't do hypnosis.'

'It seems to work, though, all this "imagining". I have been using all those visualisations and stuff for my business,' I said

'So have I!' said Mike

'Me too; and also for personal-relationship stuff,' said Pete

'Really?' said Mike 'Now there's a thought, Mr Svengali.'

Thinking back over the session, one thing I found interesting was listening to my playing and singing in isolation, stripped back from all the surroundings, just as I had experienced when listening to the playback of my vocal and guitar part in the studio.

This might have some use in my business so I recorded myself giving a presentation and became aware that I sounded rather nasal and tried out various ways of changing my tone. The one which seemed the best involved taking a deep breath and pulling in my stomach muscles. It deepened the sound of my voice, moving it away from my head giving it a feeling of gravitas. I also found drinking a little cold water gave clarity to my voice which helped it to project better.

I was gaining more confidence, with fine tunings I also noticed my voice was adapting very quickly.

Some of the techniques did seem like a mind game – but the results were so real. Initially, it confused me because I had been brought up to think of things another way – the intellectual, rational way.

However, I was taking to it all like a duck to water. Occasionally, I felt rather uncomfortable, wondering if I was deluding myself, but 'Let's face it,' I told myself, 'if it works, why bother with the analysis?'

Indeed, I greatly regretted not thinking like this before. I could have saved myself a lot of past grief – but perhaps it was due of my previous failures that these ideas seemed so attractive to me.

Pete had talked about using Grant's methods for 'personal-relationship stuff' – i.e. picking up women. This might not be so different from picking up business because, if someone likes you and finds your ideas attractive, is that any different from other forms of communication? Becoming the 'rock performer' and 'recording artist' might give me a business advantage if only in the area of having something to talk about. My ideas were buzzing with what I could do with the new-found material and I wondered what other little gems were about to come my way.

Listening to oneself, assessing one's progress and working at it has to be nurtured and it does not come naturally to me, but a good musician always strives for improvement. Perhaps this is also the key to success in business.

Chapter 10

THINGS THAT START AS A HOBBY

I suppose we were getting pleased with ourselves; we had done a few gigs and each one seemed better, in one way or another, than the last. We had played in various-sized venues and on different-sized stages. That, at first, was quite an upheaval: when we thought we had mastered the small stage, we had to deal with a big stage for a support gig at a theatre in the town. Suddenly, we had to learn to use the space again. However, something was not right. I began to notice differences in opinion over things that did not matter in the beginning.

Comments were being made about people's commitment; as, for instance, when one person in particular - Pete - repeatedly turned up late for rehearsals. Comments were also made if I had not learnt all of the lyrics for a new song. It was not as much fun as it had been; it was, dare I say, becoming serious. I decided to speak to Grant and see what he thought.

We chatted about it outside the rehearsal room. He took a deep pull on his cigarette before saying:

'Well, this time has to come in anything that starts as a hobby. Eventually, it takes on a life of it's own. When you start to get good at what you do, not everyone develops at the same speed or is committed to the same vision. People also have their own interpretations of the same ideas. If I say to you 'dog', you think of a dog; yours might be a Jack Russell, mine might be a bigger dog, such as a German Shepherd. So, if we can differ that much on a simple word, what happens when you are dealing with a concept such as a band or a business. Everyone is singing from a very different subliminal song sheet.'

This was the first time I had heard Grant refer to business, but he was 'on the nail'. Again, here was a simple but deep insight into how things work and how they would have to change. Either people's opinions or the people themselves would have change as a result of what they refer to in the business as 'musical differences'.

'What do you suggest?' I said

'I think you should at first watch and listen and then see if we can find something that will provide a mutual point of focus for the whole band. If they don't have that focus, they will leave; either by jumping or being pushed.

'It's unfortunate that things have to turn like this but, as soon as money comes into a project or hobby, or people want things to get 'more professional', then everything begins to change and the trouble starts.'

'Where are we going?' I asked.

'Anywhere you want, but you all need to be going to the same place. Sit down and think about it and watch what others are doing and see if you can read them.'

We went inside, finished the rehearsal, packed up and all went our separate ways.

BUSINESSES THAT START AS A HOBBY

My brother, Tony, who is a hobbyist-turned-businessman, is a case in point. Cars are his passion. He could be found tinkering around with any vehicle that needed repairing. He worked in a garage by day and mended motors in his own time by night. In due course, he decided that a far simpler life plan would be to turn his car-fixing into a business of his own. This was where he dropped the ball.

It became obvious, after a while, that passion can distort reality. One of Tony's main reasons for making the night job also the day job was that he had appeared to earn more money in the evening than during the day. What he hadn't foreseen was that other people are also at work during the day and so are less available, then, to bring their cars in for fixing. Furthermore, the garage he had worked for already had a customer base that they had established over a number of years while he was only at the start of building one.

In addition, his employers had been paying his taxes and so the money from moonlighting went straight into his pocket. If he had worked out his taxes and expenses and the number of working hours that were feasible, he would have realised that, to stay afloat, he had to double the prices he was charging and that, in turn, would have made him less competitive.

He was also tempted, because he liked gadgets, to overspend on machinery, and seemed unable to ask such simple questions as: 'Will I make more money by having this than by not having it?' and 'Will it pay for itself within a few months?'

In view of what Grant had said, I could see that this was a key problem for people who have a passion for something that starts as a hobby but becomes their way of making money. In a nutshell, if you want to make a living from something you are really enthusiastic about, the process has to be refined in such a way that others can get on with the work if need be, leaving you to go on a holiday – while making serious money out of what the business does. The trick is to go to work *on* your business not *in* your business.

Often, this is a tall order; many owners end up merely making themselves a tougher job instead of building a business. They have transferred working for someone else to slaving for a worse taskmaster, themselves.

I started looking at what I was doing and realised that, in the past, I had a number of projects that were not structured properly. They had been coming from the viewpoint of 'I can do *xyz* and some people may be interested in it'. Whereas good practice comes out of 'There is a demand for *xyz* and I can watch others doing something for this market whilst making a good profit margin for myself'.

Another problem is that, when you have a passion for a particular activity, you may never be able to envisage a time when you would sell the company; therefore, one of the prime ways of capitalising from the wealth of the business is lost just because of your love for it.

Tony is getting on now. He is still working his guts out fixing cars as a mobile mechanic and not charging enough for his services. I guess he is one of many talented people that are scraping a living because they have a love for what they do and who do not charge enough because they see it as ripping people off. Shame really.

Chapter 11

WHAT IS IT THAT SELLS?

We were discussing which pieces to play for a party gig that was coming up at the end of September. There were a couple of pieces in the set that we disagreed on.

'I really like that song,' said Pete.

'Yes but it is not ready yet; there is something wrong with it,' said Mike

I thought the piece was good, but it was by an unknown Australian band and, although we liked it, I was not sure that anyone in the audience would have heard it – and it was quite a tricky number to nail.

Grant was sitting quietly just watching us. 'What do you think maestro?' I asked, looking for a way to resolve this.

'Well, we are playing at a party. Does the guy whose party it is know the song?' Grant looked over at Pete.

'Probably not.' Pete shook his head.

'So he did not ask for it, then,' reasoned Grant. 'Have we included numbers that he likes?'

'Yes, we have a few,' said Pete

'In that case, if the guy does not know the song, you may as well do one of your own. Although the tune is OK, it is not a party number, and it will not get people reminiscing about the past, so it's not a number that will sell. Leave it out and concentrate on the sure-fire favourites. Besides, it is rather difficult.

'I was in a band,' he continued, 'that was doing it's own material and we all thought it sounded good, really good. However; the record company didn't see it that way, and neither did the audience; but because we had emotional capital invested in the songs, we had distorted what we thought we were hearing.

'This happens all the time in music, especially in the case of stuff that is written off as no good by the band. Then it can take the manager, a groupie or the road crew to see which one is going to be a hit. Santana hated 'Samba Pa Ti', the Police were not going to include 'Roxanne' on their first album, and Billy Joel and his band thought 'Just the Way You Are' was utter crap.

'When you have an emotional involvement in creative material, it will distort your idea of how it will sell. It needs someone else to put you in the picture.

'Find what sells, what adds to the set; forget about what you like. Go for the one that creates ripples and builds interest and excitement in your fans – and do that.'

Grant played the riff from 'Under Pressure' by Queen on two open strings and smiled broadly: 'This is a nice riff, but it will never sell because it is too simple!' he chuckled to himself.

'OK, point taken!' Pete said

We looked at the set list and decided to make some more changes and, after a while, it looked very impressive (and a lot easier than the previous version). It was wall-to-wall party music which, you could tell, was going to go like a rocket.

WHAT IS IT THAT SELLS? FIND OUT, GO GET IT AND THEN SELL
IT!

I had a call from a friend, Bob, who was trying to set up in business as a guitar teacher. He said that he was trying to grow the business but that it was proving difficult to find customers.

I asked him what was he was doing about advertising. He explained that he had spent a lot on adverts in the local press, after which a handful of people had contacted him regarding lessons and some even turned up for a few; however, the numbers had dwindled.

'I think that I am attracting the wrong people,' he said

'So are these people who don't want to play guitar then?'

'Well of course they do; they're answering my ad, aren't they?' he answered

'But you told me they were the wrong people!' I could see he was making an interesting statement that was probably the root of the problem.

'What I mean is they do not want to learn properly.'

I knew that I had hit on the crux of the matter. 'What do you mean by "learn properly"?'

'Well, they need to learn the scales and the chords and to hold the guitar properly and they have to be able to read music.'

I was beginning to see what was going on here.

'Let me ask you something,' I said. 'Do you know what they want to do?'

'Oh, I guess lots of them want to play grunge and new metal' Tony said.

'In that case, mate, you know what sells so go and sell it to them. And then, as you go on from there, slip in the technique and the scales – but do it with the material they like.'

I told Bob the story of what happened to us in the band and how Grant explained about crowd-focused music. During the telling, Bob started to see that it was not about the 'right' audience, it was about getting to the audience that he was already attracting and developing that by working with their likes.

I considered how this self-centred view point seems to be evident in many business ideas that come up. They are often ideas that feature high on the profile of one person, the guy whose idea it is. You only have to watch a programme such as

'Dragon's Den' to see that many of the pitches assume that the customer will see the benefit that the business can bestow on them but often there is no demand for that product.

These people need to go out and open their eyes and ears to the outside world, and shut down their own internal desires and interests, and focus only on the customer that they will make their idea really fly.

This is such simple common sense – but common sense is not that common. It does need someone from outside, someone with no emotional investment in your creative project, to come in and tell you what they see.

What Bob had was potentially a good teaching practice if he got customers learning while playing the music they wanted to play. They were showing him that he was getting it wrong by voting with their feet.

Chapter 12

GROUP THE SONGS INTO SECTIONS SO THAT THEY ARE EASY
TO PRACTISE

'Being systematic as you build a play list for a band is very important. It saves a lot of time when you practise and also makes learning easier.'

Grant was showing us that, instead of the songs in list being a moveable feast, if they were put together in blocks, we could move them around. By grouping them in threes and fours, we would always know which order they came in; and then, if we changed the set, we would replace one block with another.

This got around the problem of the awkward gaps in between songs. We had noticed that, as the set progressed, sometimes it was difficult to keep the numbers we had well rehearsed.

'In the same way that you worked on getting on and off the stage smoothly, so we need to ensure that the songs flow from one to another seamlessly and, when there are interludes, that these are planned.'

Grant was explaining to us that many famous examples of seemingly spontaneous 'stage business', such as cigarette lighters being waived and flowers being thrown from the audience, started life as 'set-up jobs'.

Grant continued, 'There is no such thing as an unrehearsed improvisation; for a good improvisation, things are so well rehearsed that they seem spontaneous.'

As we played using these blocks of songs, our performance got tighter and we looked more professional.

Grant explained the reason why the Beatles were so good as a band was because, during their Hamburg tours, they played several times a day for an hour or so at a time and amassed thousands of hours of playing time. They, often played repeated the same song or else repeated the same chords patterns but with different lyrics as is the way with twelve-bar patterns such as rock'n'roll and blues that they are the same song with different words.

Grant explained that if you added up the time that the Beatles had played together before becoming famous they must have clocked up many thousands of hours.

There is, as he explained it, an unintended consequence to putting material together like this in that there is a shift in the way that we think about the music and this is what tightens the set up.

'The spaces between songs can be reason for the loss of momentum in the performance it's as it gives the audience an excuse to sit down. If you are a band that want the crowd to be up and dancing, then do not stop between songs – keep them on their feet.'

As work with Grant went on, it became clear that it was not the songs – nor the notes – that were the focus, it was how you played them. Always, the secret of a good performance lay deep in the delivery and the surroundings in which they were played.

'So much of this is a gut feeling and impossible to put into specific-enough words. The real answer is that people vote with their feet: "Yes" is they get up and dance and "No" is when they get up and leave.

'OK, let's go through the numbers again.' Grant counted in the next song.

MAKE SYSTEMS THAT SIMPLIFY PROCESSES AND USE THEM

When I first left school I worked in a bank. In those days this particular bank had it's cheque-clearing done by the National Westminster Bank and, although 'my' bank was in the process of change (which would make it into a larger bank in its own right), that had not happened as yet.

I took over the foreign-exchange till and observed there were numerous forms that were replicating one another. So I suggested we did the following: take a copy of the form used as the order (in those days we did not carry the foreign currency; that had to be shipped in via head office) and, after filling in one form, everyone else used a copy of that.

I got the OK for this change which made the ordering far more efficient – in large part because less forms to fill in meant less room for error as you only had to make sure the first form was filled in correctly, remember this was before computerisation.

When you are using a system which simplifies a process, even if it is merely for opening the post, it can make a massive difference to your time efficiency.

I remember when working for a shipping company that I used to pick up a file, then read it, then put it down, then later pick it up again and then move it to another part of the desk. After a while, I realised I was double- and triple-handling pieces of paper, so I created a system using a diary and notes attached to the files with its progress written on the front. I knew exactly what the situation was with any job at any time. This simple idea greatly reduced the amount of time required to do that job.

What surprised me, however, was I did not follow the same strategies at home where, as a result, I was far less organised.

When Grant had spoken of arranging our music into blocks, I could see the logic. It meant all we needed to rehearse were either the new blocks which were coming into the next set or the blocks containing things that had gone wrong at a previous gig – but not the whole set.

There are probably many things we do which can, with careful thought, be streamlined, thus freeing up lots of time, For me, this was true of reading the post or processing some types of jobs but, as I started to think about it, it was true of many other things from bookkeeping to doing the washing up or contacting customers or doing exercises or practising the guitar – in fact, for pretty much everything I could think of.

Even in a business where systems are in place to streamline procedures, people will compensate and fill the time that has been saved by technology – so these procedures constantly need revisiting and revising.

Chapter 13

THERE IS ALWAYS SOMETHING YOU CAN LEARN FROM A GREAT PLAYER

Grant complemented me, 'You are playing with real soul there's a message in what you're doing. I have a friend that you might like to see; he is someone you could learn a lot from.'

At first, I took this as rather a strange complement and it left me with a few conflicting feelings, but I agreed that I would like to see the guy play.

A week or so later, we turned up at a small theatre where he was performing in a band called The Boogie Brothers. I thought the name would set the mood for the evening; however, when they kicked into the set, the young guitarist played some subtle stuff and was instantly noticeable as being very soulful.

The first solo blew my socks off. The sound, the timing and the feel were all fabulous and, as the set went on, he got better and better. I was beginning to think that my guitar should be placed in its case and locked away because I was not worthy.

The Boogie Brothers had really thought their set out well and they avoided the trap that most fall into where, after the first four numbers, everything starts to sound the same.

Grant said we could catch up with them at the end of the gig and he would introduce me.

We went backstage and Grant signalled to the guitarist who smiled broadly at Grant and came over.

'Hi Grant, good to see you, thanks for coming', he looked at me and Grant introduced the guitarist as Josh.

'I enjoyed your playing, Josh, you are a very gifted.' I said

Josh smiled: 'If you practiced as much as I do you would be too,' he said

'I doubt that; you are so fast and you have such a great ear.' I seemed to be coming up with reasons why I was not as good and could not be.

'Let me tell you a secret; it is 10,000 hours.' He looked at me, still smiling. 'I was not that good and then Grant said to me, 'Do you want to be the best?' and I said I did, and then he told me: Practise for 10,000 hours and you will be!'

'But you must have the ability to start with,' I said

'We all have the ability to start with. It is all about practise. When you are prepared to put in the time, everything else comes your way. It is almost like your brain changes. I did not believe that at first but now I know it's true. There was a famous cellist who said "Genius is 1% inspiration and 99% percent perspiration", isn't that right Grant?'

'So, can I be as good as you?' I said

'Yes, put in the time, focus on what you want and go for it' Josh looked across at a beautiful young blonde who walked over. 'Ok guys, it was great to see you both. I will catch up for a beer but I must be off now. I have another pressing engagement.' He winked.

I turned to Grant; 'He made me feel like giving up – he was so superb – but now I feel really encouraged.'

'I remember a time,' said Grant, 'when he could not even play in time, so I know what he is saying is true. Now, he plays several hours a day and, within three years, Josh has become what you see now. Cool, eh?'

I HAVE MET A FEW GREAT BUSINESSMEN IN MY TIME

I know a few people who really seem able to make money like there is no tomorrow, but what has struck me about all of them is they are quite happy to tell you how they did it and how you could do the same.

They can also take an idea that you have missed then extrapolate the idea out so that they can produce the relevant figures – first small and then big.

For instance they may say: 'This will cost you x per unit and there are so many thousand that you can sell with a y mark up so, therefore, you should be able to make z sort of profit.' They don't even need to do this on the back of an envelope. It is all in their heads. It seems to come with the territory of the entrepreneur.

What I have learnt from most of them is that they are switched into this type of thinking all of the time. It's as if they are doing the 10,000 hours of practise at being a businessman, and maybe that's what makes them successful.

They often have things go wrong, but the rule seems to be: 'Have enough successes to make the money to cover the failures, and more besides.'

There is much to be learnt and again, as with my experience with the guitarist, Josh, meeting someone who has 'the touch' can make you feel like giving up and getting an ordinary job working for someone else.

The motto from one of these businessmen was: 'Do not go to work *in* your job, but go to work *on* your job and go to work on *you*.' Build the expertise, be a learning machine and develop the skills that you need to get the edge over the competition and then, through your ability to perform, destroy the competition.

Make people stand in awe of you because of your brilliance at solving their problems for them.

Apart from the element of beginners' luck that can happen in business, generally the innate ability to realise opportunity comes from experience which, over time, has become deeply ingrained in the mind. When triggered, it reappears as instinctive action. By then, the person using this skill may have forgotten the processes that created it.

I have asked friends about their successes in business and how they achieved them and often the first response was, 'I don't know; it just seemed to go right'. But as you dig deeper, you can see they had a plan of action which may have been so ingrained it was hidden to them.

It seems, therefore, that the motto is, 'Practise until you forget'. At that stage, you are working instinctively and the ideas and the opportunities seem to come at you from everywhere because you have trained yourself to see and be aware.

Chapter 14

HOW TO WRITE A SONG; START WITH A FLOW OF SOMEONE
ELSE'S IDEAS.

We decided that it would be good to write a couple of songs of our own. It was great doing other people's material but we thought it might be good to slip some of our own into the set, just for the fun of it. After a few attempts at writing lyrics and putting sequences of chords together, we realised that this was not as easy as we first imagined.

We played through one idea which was the best of the bunch but it did not seem to be going anywhere.

Grant just followed instructions and did not say anything, but something about this didn't feel right.

'Do you songwrite Grant,' asked Pete

'Yes, I do,' Grant answered

'Come on then, what is wrong with what we are doing? What is the secret of this art form?'

'Firstly, it is not an art form, it is a craft,' Grant looked at everyone. 'You see, if you are waiting for the great ideas to come, they probably won't; what you need is a plan.'

'If you are a carpenter, what you do is a craft. You can make the same piece of furniture again and again because you have a plan and you are not waiting for inspiration. Songwriting is like that. What you need is a flow of ideas, so start with something that works. In other words, use other people's ideas.' Grant picked up a pen and the pad of paper with the lyrics on.

'Start with a set of chords that you know work because they have already proved themselves in a song, and then move them around a bit and experiment. Next, use the song from which you took the chords as a template. The structure of that song will answer the questions that arise as you write. For instance, 'What comes next?' will be answered in the original. It might be the bridge or the chorus or a solo . . .

'The reason this happens,' Grant continued, 'is simple. A piece of music works because it follows a plan that is familiar and that is why we like it. What we enjoy in a song is mostly about what we find familiar, and that is true of most things in life.

'The great artists rarely created something new. They often took two styles of music that already worked and blended them together to give the illusion of something different. The Beatles did it, Led Zeppelin did it, Bob Dylan did it and now you can do it!' Grant took the chords of a Neil Young song and moved them around a bit on the sheet of paper.

'Make a start with this and see how you get on with the structure; then we will look at how to write lyrics and later we will look at how to add the magic dust.'

'OK Grant, thanks for that; but do you not think that sometimes people do create works of art in music?' Pete asked

'Yes they do; when a carpenter makes furniture, every now and again one piece is special – but it is still a chair. It is functional and it does exactly what you expect. Often, art does something that you do not expect. Remember that you are in the area of pop music and so you want it to do what you expect; if not write some modern jazz.' Grant smiled.

'Fair enough. I suppose we should get on and write a rock classic,' I said

'Exactly.' Grant handed me the pad.

START A RESTAURANT, ROAST A YAK AND SERVE IT WITH YOGURT.

Later that week, a friend of mine, Chris phoned and, during our chat, he mentioned new business idea. He said that he was looking to open a restaurant in the town and that he was going to do something really different because all the places to eat were 'much of a muchness'.

'So what sort of thing do you want to do?' I asked.

'Well, I have seen a franchise for a Mongolian restaurant that looks good,' Chris replied.

'What? In our dysfunctional town they wouldn't know anything about Mongolia or its food, even if Genghis Khan hit them around the head with a Yak,' I said.

Chris went on to extol the virtues of the franchise and how well it had taken off in other places. I was still sceptical.

After the call, I thought over Chris's wish to start a restaurant that was 'different'. It seemed to me the reason why all the restaurants in our town were fairly traditional was because they worked.

In my opinion Tom's best course of action was, first, to find out what really was successful in our town and then to look at incorporating into that format some of the new business aspects of other restaurant businesses which worked elsewhere.

By starting with a successful restaurant which people felt familiar and then introducing elements successful in other towns, he would be creating a hybrid which had the virtues of appearing new but, in fact, being pretty 'safe'.

In the town, we already had a couple of Gastro pubs, a Chinese restaurant, a Thai, two Indians, a Chinese take-away and three pubs that served pub grub. There were also a number of café's plus a sandwich bar, a kebab shop and a chippy.

Our town was, therefore, obviously the place to go if you were hungry; so, no reason for it not to be good for another restaurant.

Indeed, the location Chris was looking at had, for a long time, been the site of one restaurant or another but all had been unable to survive. Interestingly, because all the others places that I have just mentioned had been thriving for years. This location, by contrast, had been home to a Mexican and then an American-style burger restaurant, then some sort of flouncy, rather nondescript 'English' and now – potentially –

a Mongolian. The restaurants on the other sites in town were very obvious establishments and that was the thing which stood out: the formula.

Start with something that works and then add other elements that are proven. Maybe mix and match a little, but keep to what works. If you come up with something totally original, no one will use you and your business will die *because* it is different. Remember, the only thing a restaurant really needs to survive is a hungry crowd and the hungry crowd will go to the place they know.

So, as with music, familiarity seems to be the driving force. Understandably we need a little bit of difference to spice it up – but only a little of the unexpected. Maybe the Mongolian restaurant is a steppe too far.

Chapter 15

COULD PLAYING AN INSTRUMENT MAKE YOU LIVE LONGER?

While driving to work one day, I was listening to a piece on the radio about singing or playing an instrument being beneficial to your health. When I reached the office, I looked for some research on the internet. One thing that caught my attention was, by means of a simple test, scientists reckon they can predict the life expectancy of an individual. The test had revealed that a person who was happy at work and in the rest of their life could add five years, whereas someone who was unhappy might well lose five years. A 10-year difference!

That evening, whilst I was playing the guitar, I thought carefully about how I felt. For me playing was acting as a stress buster. The easiest thing for me to do to relax was to bash a few chords or just ramble around some lead.

At the next rehearsal, I talked to Grant about the research.

'When I started playing the guitar,' he said 'I was very mixed up. I didn't know what I wanted to do with my life and I suppose I just fell into the idea of playing the bass. I still get my acoustic guitar out to play a few chords when I want to chill, though. It made a massive difference to how I felt and gave a boost to my personality by building my confidence. I ended up performing in front of people at concerts and, after a while, I got involved working with a number of different bands because, as you know, bass players are thin on the ground. It wasn't long before I was touring around the country and then around Europe. So, music wasn't just good for my health, it actually gave me a reason to live. Indeed, I can tell you lots of stories of people who have got their life back on track by learning to play music.

'A couple of guys were imprisoned for theft but, while they were inside, they learnt the guitar and started to write songs. It changed them by giving them a new way of expressing themselves and it really healed them. These guys are still going straight and are doing stuff like getting kids involved in music. We need more things like that happening'.

Grant looked into the distance and shook his head. 'Music and the arts generally are so undervalued in this society, and I think it is to the detriment of all.'

I had never really thought of music like that; it had just been a hobby and fairly expendable, but since I had become deeply involved in playing in the band, it was different. The feeling of music becoming very important had crept up on me. I hadn't had a troubled childhood; in fact, looking back at it, I had been very lucky. However, for many their work becomes all-encompassing and that is where music (and all the arts) becomes a way of breaking that up and giving you back quality time while putting anger and frustration to good use in the music you play.

Maybe this is where I had got to. I was bored and music had adding something new to me.

Grant smiled: 'So, I am not so sure if music will make you live longer, but life won't seem so bloody boring!'

I agreed.

COULD MUSIC MEAN THAT YOU WORK BETTER?

If you played an instrument, or at least had a life outside your job, would you work more productively?

There seems to be an attitude among some business owners of wanting to own their employees. I have seen this in professions such as the law and accountancy where firms work new graduates to exhaustion, expecting them to stay late into the evening as a sign of commitment. The unspoken and unwritten rule is, if you want to be viewed for promotion – or even to be sure of keeping your job – you need to be seen to be staying late.

It has long been the way of the medical profession where the junior doctors are worked to total burnout as if this is a right of passage that has to be endured like a badge of honour.

Is it possible we could get more out of people if they were encouraged to be creative? It seemed clear to me that playing music with others involves many aspects of working together. I wasn't sure that getting people to be creative would necessarily help people with their work; I felt it would depend on the job. However I met a person who changed my mind.

I was looking to design some office space, and I had been recommended an architect to do the plans so I organised an appointment.
After entering the firm's offices and talking to the secretary, I was aware of a very jovial but also hard-working atmosphere throughout the building. I was shown into the main office to meet the boss and there, in the corner, was a guitar with an amp and various effects pedals.

'Oh, you play guitar!'. Obviously there was a delighted ring to my voice.

'Yes, do you?' came the reply.

'Was it that obvious from the tone of my voice?' I said.

The conversation then went into the world of music and we both spoke about our bands and the music which influenced us and how much fun it was. After several minutes of musical chat we eventually got around to talking business, we now felt like old friends. The rapport began as an interest in music but developed into more of a friendship because, I suppose, we were alike in our interests and therefore predisposed to like one another.

The architect, whose name was Alistair, said that the guitar was always a talking point for visitors. However, for himself, when things got difficult, he plugged it in and played Stones or Zeppelin riffs. It always made him feel better, and it really got him out of his problems by changing his focus. He felt having a relaxed atmosphere in the office helped to lighten the mood and gave a space for creativity.

I left the building and had a chuckle about the strange serendipity following me concerning music. Almost as soon as I posed a musical question, circumstances would arise and conspire to reveal something.

I found someone who was using music in their business life to help themselves in their day-to-day work, fair enough this was rather extreme as not everyone can play in the office but the staff had music on. I resolved that I should actively take these lessons and applying them directly to my personal and business life.

Chapter 16

WHO OWNS THE PA? WE ALL DO!

We had agreed to buy a Public Address system (PA), as up to now we had been borrowing one from a friend. Getting big speakers and a decent mixer would help us play the bigger halls without having to hire in equipment. Grant had suggested that we should 'mic up' the bass drum, as it would help with the overall sound, so we chose to buy the PA collectively.

Grant also pointed out that we should think carefully about what happened if one of us left. Did he forfeit his share in the PA or would we pay him off? What would happen if someone was kicked out or if the group split?

'You see, when you are all happy, these things are not considered; and yet, in time, they will have to be looked at because these issues which seem unimportant now will become very important later.'

We thought about this for a while and one of us suggested the PA should be purchased out of the gigging funds. As we had earned money from the gigs, it seemed appropriate that we paid for the equipment out of the earnings and therefore removed the feeling that we had individual share. We also thought that if the group was to split, then the PA should be sold and the proceeds were to be shared between the members.

We could have gone the way of most about-to be wed couples: they are in love and they believe that they will be together until the end and therefore the idea of discussing the sharing of their possessions, should they divorce, does not feature on the radar. Being in a band, is like being in a marriage in a strange sort of way. Indeed, being in a business is like being married, especially when you realise that you spend more time with your work colleagues than your spouse.

Pete suggested that we ought to think about who was going to carry the large speakers, etc, and that we had to make sure we all contributed to the lugging around and setting up.

We set to work drafting the key points of funding the equipment, ownership and sharing the workload and within a couple of days we had these signed up as an agreement.

It was strange that, after we sat down and had this discussion, a couple of us heard various stories of groups splitting and selling the gear and people arguing over who owned what. Perhaps making an agreement like this might have saved them some of the heartbreak.

In a few years, we would have a van and a lighting rig, all of which would be owned by us. We would be shareholders unless we left by our own volition. If we were kicked out, then our share would be reimbursed to us at the current market valuation for the equipment. However, that was for another day.

Grant wrapped it up: 'All such agreements are flawed to some extent. However the idea is to lessen the possibilities of future problems arising by clearing the ground first, then you can focus on the music.'

WHO OWNS THE WEBSITE? THEY DO!

An old colleague of mine, Dan, started up a series of summer schools in order to encourage people to start playing music with others.

It began as a rough plan with various people pitching in to help start the project. Dan, who was a teacher, had the mainframe of ideas. Jeff was the business brain behind it and got the company established. Paul a bass player had set up the website and did the website design and they were also joined by a small team of teachers.

The first year was a success. They broke even and everything seemed to work pretty well. However, it became more and more obvious that Paul had his own ideas about the school and its teaching programme. Various members of the team had started to question his teaching ability and his communication skills, especially as a couple of customers had complained about his attitude during the course.

To cut a long story short, Paul left, along with another team member, to set up a rival company. But what he also did was redirect all the traffic from the old site to his new website along with the client information, even though Dan's company owned the data base.

Paul was able to do this because he owned the original website address and because this had been arranged in the honeymoon period when they were all friends no one had questioned the way this had been set up. Obviously, then, no one was looking at the possibility that someone would leave.

The damage had not been great but it was inconvenient and took a couple of months to rectify.

We need to look into the dark side of partnerships because things will go wrong, especially when we are working with people who we do not know that well. Within a short while, Dan's company replaced Paul and brought in some new teachers who proved far superior and they moved to a better venue. At this point, everything took off because of the change in their profile. This was a direct result of their looking closely at what had happened and responding to it.

By contrast, the other company more or less carried on with what they had been doing before. Although they wanted change they did not change at all!

Problems were created because of an error in the way the ownership (in this case ownership of website) was set up and, although it eventually led to a better situation for the parent company, it would have been best avoided.

Dan succeeded because the company were able to adapt, but not everyone is this fortunate.

Chapter 17

WHEN DRIVING THE CAR CAN BE THE ANSWER

When we started I thought we would be just playing for fun with the odd gig here and there. What happened was we became a tight regular gigging band – all be it we were mostly doing covers (which was) was good enough for us. However, it seemed I now needed to raise my game and, therefore, I decided to take some lessons and asked Grant to teach me.

Although I had known Grant as a bass player, he also taught guitar and I thought this would be a good place to start because I liked what he did and said.

I turned up at Grant's house. He already had a cup of tea waiting for me and we sat down and chatted for a while. I explained that I had a few technical things which I could not seem to get on top of (one of them was a relaxed rhythm pattern) and my ideas seemed to be the same all of the time.

Grant listened and then reached over and found a track on the CD player. He said I should cover the strings over with my left hand on the fretboard so I could achieve a percussive sound.

He started playing a Seventies funk track, which sounded a bit like Earth Wind and Fire, and he then told me to play along as if I was joining in with the percussion.

I started strumming, and it was pretty basic to begin with, but, as he talked to me, it became more relaxed and more inventive.

'In a minute I will stop the music but you will carry on strumming. Remember to feel it and listen to what you are playing'.

I did exactly as he said and it sounded good. Then he instructed me to play some chords with the same rhythm. 'Wow, this sounds really good! What happened?' I asked. Grant explained:

'You have files in your head that have complex rhythms in them, the ones which you play when waiting at traffic lights. You tap them out on the steering wheel and they are much better than the ones you play on the guitar! Because they are relaxed and creative, not the rather dull patterns that you have learnt for the guitar. All we did was to find them by playing along with the song, and then we removed the song but added the chords. So we just moved the file across from one part of your mind to another'.

We went on to playing different styles of music and, each time, I came up with a different rhythmic pattern. I was amazed at how varied and exciting 'new' ideas were. This was in complete contrast to what I usually did when I played.

When I left the lesson, I was so highly charged; I worked and worked on the ideas, coming up with lots of variations for different styles. What a difference! I could not believe that something so simple could be so transforming.

FINDING A FILE AND MOVING IT OVER

What other things could I use this technique for, to fix or improve things? Did I have skills in one area in my life which could fix problems in other aspect? I started to look at situations in my work life and personal life needing improvement.

One thing which struck me was how I was very time conscious in certain tasks and not in others. As I have said, when I started work, I used to pick up a letter or an invoice and then read it, then put it down and later pick it up again, and then move it to another part of the desk, which is time wasting. However, I did not follow the same strategies at home where I was, therefore, more organised.

This was evident when Grant had said I already had better ideas for rhythm in my head, yet I was not using them for playing guitar, only for drumming on a steering wheel. So, the first stage of improving my playing was a matter of my making better use of information.

There are probably many things which, by breaking old patterns and bringing one in from a different activity can make one more effective.

What happens in one business sector which does not happen in another business? Is there something which is normal practice in one industry that is not routine in another would help another increase trade.

I remember reading the work of Jay Abraham, an American entrepreneurial guru, who had worked in various jobs as a young man and who then made a real impact by mixing different tricks of the various trade moving them from one business model to another.

I know many books, have looked at famous historical people, from Genghis Khan to Gandhi, examining their ways of doing things and translating them into different management styles. I am sure that these management styles do not include massacring whole cities or attempting to make your employees spin their own textiles.

For me, strategies which worked elsewhere that I could 'move over' then reapply seemed exciting, partly because many ideas were my own in the first place I was not attempting to be someone else.

In my case, I was a reasonable artist and when I painted a picture I could 'see' the image on the canvas before I started to draw. This ability to hallucinate the picture worked for my artwork and to some extent I did this for business but not in a controlled way.

However using this for a new business idea and I noticed I could really 'picture the outcome' which in turn helped to develop the thoughts in a logical way to achieve the end goal.

Making the pictures run like a film helped as well, as if moving images 'powered up' the changes I was making and provided the sense that they were happening ('running') in real time. There was a sense of change happening as I did this which helped to motive me.

This is still very much 'work in progress' like discovering parts of one's mind which have been locked away.

Chapter 18

TECHNOLOGY CAN MAKE US LOOSE THE MUSIC

I was looking at Grant's musical equipment. His guitar and amplifier had both certainly seen some action and, although he did have effects pedals, they too were well used.

'Is there any reason why you only use old gear – or is it just the cost?'

'I have, in fact, tried lots of amps and guitars', Grant responded, 'but this stuff works really well and I like the sound it makes.'

'I saw this amazing amp the other day and it had all the effects in it . . . what do you think? 'Before I had finished describing the make and model, Grant was shaking his head,

'Don't get that, if the amp or the effects go wrong, you will loose everything. You should keep the effects separately and carry a spare amp, spare guitar and a spare overdrive pedal; then, what ever happens you are covered. You must have a fall-back position for technology failure.'

'Apart from that, the more you get used to your instruments in their purest form, the better you will get to know the sound and the feel of them. The problem is, of course, that although technology starts as our slave, it ends up becoming our master.'

Grant patiently explained that we need to be very careful to control the tools we use in making in music:

'A good song is a good song not because it has an interesting sound effect in it. That might make it sound better but will not make a bad song into a classic. Also, technology can leave us in serious trouble when it goes wrong – rather like some form of life support being switched off. '

Grant lectured me about the secrets of great music being the same now as it was when all instruments were acoustic it is our response to the sound not the sound itself and because of that often the more 'natural' a sound was the more it resonated with us.

Technology has always been important to us from the day that we understood fire and made tools to make and catch things. The problem is that when we become dependant on it we can become vulnerable so we need to have a fall back position to cover for the rare moments when things pack up as in Murphy's Law they will happen when we are unprepared.

'There is nothing wrong with it but we must beware of its limitations and its flaws in that way we get the best of both worlds.' Grant plugged in the guitar, 'You see I love electricity!'

TECHNOLOGY CAN PRODUCE MONSTERS

A few years ago, an architect friend of mine was working on a case which was in dispute and was preparing documents on behalf of his clients. He had received an email from the other party and was preparing to forward it, complete with his comments – which contained highly confidential information - to his clients. However, he accidentally hit the reply-to-all button, thus sending a copy to the party that they were in dispute with.

As he hit the button, he realised what he had done but there was no way of getting the email back and all he could do was inform his clients. They were none too pleased and were fully prepared to sue him for damages, which would have totalled somewhere in the region of one million pounds.

He was sick with worry but, in fact, it worked to his advantage because, as it was viewed as a form of disclosure, the case was resolved in his client's favour.

In pre-computer days, this would have involved sending of a letter to the wrong address and been far less likely. Due to the ease of technology, a simple action can cause results out of all proportion to the error.

Unfortunately, while we have become so reliant on technology, we have also become blinded to what can happen when we act unthinkingly. Our dependency leads us – sleepwalking – into problems.

Many years ago, I worked for a shipping company where the shipments involved dealing with complex letters of credit for which the bank stipulated the exact content and wording of the paperwork. Therefore, if the address on the letter of credit had an error in it, the documents also had to contain that error otherwise the bank would have withheld payment.

I took over work for an Indian shipment that had been running for a number of years. The practice was to start, each time, with the original file and then copy the paperwork and change the details as necessary. Over time, the documentation got bigger and bigger because people thought, 'Well, that was needed last time so we will send it again.' No one appeared to check the letter of credit to see what was required so, therefore, the were lots of unnecessary letters and invoices going which all still had to be correct. I was able to throw away half of the existing paperwork on the next job.

There was no system for checking what was happening with the ongoing orders and because of the new technology (which at the time was the photocopier) the number of letters and invoices supplied grew with each job, it was just easy to copy what had been done before.

So in all situations be very careful of the downside created by technology.

Chapter 19

KNOWING WHEN IT IS TIME.

Pete, Mike, Grant and I had been playing together for about a year and, during that time, we had become very professional, playing a wide rage of music with a few of our own numbers thrown into the mix when the gig situations were right.

We had some great prospects for gigs during the following year and were, therefore, somewhat taken aback when Grant told us of his plans to leave.

'I am going away for a while, on tour with a friend's band, so I have trained up someone who can step in and take my place.'

We were not expecting this and, anyway, we knew that Grant had lots of gigs and sessions planned, apart from playing with us.

'It will be a shame to loose you, Grant,' I said. 'We have learnt so much from you and come such a long way.' Everybody agreed.

'I have enjoyed working with you guys immensely and you have become a great line-up, but it is my time to move on. I am not sure I can be of much more use to you because you know what to do now.'

'I'm sure there is much more you can tell us about the business and music,' Pete said.

Grant looked at him: 'When I was younger, I had a guitar teacher who was amazing – an inspiration to me. He was a classical player and he taught me how to make the music happen and how to put emotion into the music. One day, he said that he could not teach me anything else because he had taught me all he knew. I was very upset at the time but he was adamant. He was right, but it took me a long time to understand.'

'So who is the new guy?' I said.

'Martin, he is young but very good. He has seen us play a few times, he likes the material, he needs the money and he is as keen as mustard. You will like him.'

So, it was agreed, the following week, Martin would join us and that was it.

It was strange seeing Grant leave. It was like watching an old sage walking out of the door. He turned, and said goodbye, yet reassuring us he would be in touch when he got back. But, looking at me straight in the eye, he smiled and said: ' I am leaving for the west with my ox.'

Geoff had been working hard over the past few years on a little project that now seemed to be going well and making some good returns.

He was a turnaround artist – someone who takes on struggling businesses (or organisations) and revives them. In Geoff's case, he bought up small companies, restructured them so that they were operating successfully and then sold them on.

He had, in the past, completed several ventures including a haulage firm and a bakery. This was all far removed from the financial job in the city that he had held for a number of years, but he said he needed a change and turning around small ventures was fun and presented different challenges.

Geoff and I were friends from school and we met up every now and again to touch base. This time it was for a coffee at his office.

Geoff was taking about his latest project – a small outfit dealing with the storage of high-performance cars – which gave him the interest of dealing with Porsches and Ferrari's and getting paid for it! The only problem was that changing the ethos in the company to being more businesslike was going to prove tough for everyone. He knew he couldn't take any prisoners but hoped, once they realised he was there to get the company back in shape, that people would respond positively. And, so far, this was going well.

The employees had to take a drop in pay for a few months but, as he had shown them he had not taken any money for the past eight months, they seemed to be happy with the deal. In everyone's mind was the desire to keep the business going because everyone shared the same passion for elite cars.

Geoff explained, in these ventures, knowing when to sell, thus realising the profit, was the important part of the equation.

In the past, with the haulage firm, he had nearly got it wrong. If he had sold a few months later, he would have made no money from his investment because a problem with fuel prices and a dip in trade would have badly affected the sale.

I was impressed with the wide variety of projects he had chosen and wondered if it took time to get up to speed in a new sector.

'Not really; there are some things I have to get to know but my focus is not the functioning of the job; that is for someone else. My focus is all about the business, the cost base, the profit margin and looking to expand and add value. In the end, with these ventures, you have to leave otherwise you end up with just another job, and I don't want that.

'How do you know when to leave?' I asked him.

'In the end, it is a gut feeling. I begin to smell the money and that is when I need to sell'. Geoff replied

'So can you sell it yet?' I pressed him.

'Not yet; I have a few more things to set in place – and then I will be getting near. But I will know when it is time to leave.' Geoff nodded his head.

'You see, to make a profit and get a good deal you need to be able to walk away. If you fall in love with what you do you can lose out. The secret is to detach and then you will make money.' Geoff smiled.

TESTIMONIALS

"Full of useful insights, fresh ideas and new perspectives on how the lessons learned from playing music can be incorporated into creative business thinking."
Tony Skinner, RGT Director.

Do not underestimate the power of music. This book shows the direct parallel with modern day business and how interaction, communication and empathy can lead to success whilst having an empowering effect upon your well-being in all walks of life; Vic Hyland succinctly portraits this. Pick up an instrument, you won't regret it.

Mike Kilgour, Director MKA Architects (and part time guitarist!)

Music is a divine and wondrous gift that has been the soundtrack to our lives since the first drum was beaten. It puts us in touch with ourselves, with nature and with the workings of the mind be it in business or something deeper.
What better way to wake up to our selves and to our possibilities than through the message of music? When all around us seems to be crumbling, music tells us all is well, it always has been, and it always will be.
Thank you, Vic, for your music, and for this wonderful tale.

Shazzie, TV Presenter and Author

"And when the song is played well, we all sing together!
Thanks Vic, this is a great book with beautiful messages for musicians and business folk alike to take their skills and craft to the next level.
Breathe in, use all your senses to experience the difference and let the good times roll!
Jo James, Business Coach at www.amberlife.com and rhythm guitarist!

ABOUT THE AUTHOR

Vic Hyland is nationally known for his educational work with the guitar, and his research work into creativity in music. He is also an international examiner for the Registry of Guitar Tutors.

Vic's guitar playing has also been likened to a mixture of Hendrix, Santana and Jeff Beck and his voice to that of Sting. He is a prolific and versatile songwriter often creating a hybrid from differing influences, which can be experienced on his many CDs.

He has also had a considerable influence on many up and coming musicians, through nurturing new talent and also delivering his regular lectures on the music business. These include the use of Neuro-Linguistic Programming (which Vic learnt from Richard Bandler and the hypnotist Paul McKenna) and ideas developed from various techniques such as Accelerated Learning and Lateral Thinking.

His interest in the consciousness and creativity area has led to the book Art of Practice and the CD Creativity and Health that deals with the areas of learning and the problems with education within society. Vic is also a director of '440 Music Ltd' a company that runs the Bluescampuk summer schools.

Further information about his work can be found at www.vichyland.com and www.bluescampuk.co.uk